# DOGS SET VII

# SCHNOODLES

Jill C. Wheeler
ABDO Publishing Company

# visit us at
# www.abdopublishing.com

Published by ABDO Publishing Company, 8000 West 78th Street, Edina, Minnesota 55439. Copyright © 2008 by Abdo Consulting Group, Inc. International copyrights reserved in all countries. No part of this book may be reproduced in any form without written permission from the publisher. The Checkerboard Library™ is a trademark and logo of ABDO Publishing Company.

Printed in the United States.

Cover Photo: Chelle Rohde Calbert/www.designerdoggies.com
Interior Photos: Animals Animals p. 19; AP Images p. 17; Chelle Rohde Calbert/www.designerdoggies.com p. 5; iStockphoto pp. 13, 15; Peter Arnold pp. 7, 9; Pierce Schnoodles@www.pierceschnoodles.com pp. 11, 18, 21

Editors: Heidi M.D. Elston, Megan M. Gunderson
Art Direction: Neil Klinepier

## Library of Congress Cataloging-in-Publication Data

Wheeler, Jill C., 1964-
  Schnoodles / Jill C. Wheeler.
     p. cm. --  (Dogs. Set VII)
  Includes index.
  ISBN 978-1-59928-966-3
  1.  Schnoodle--Juvenile literature.  I. Title.

  SF429.S378W44 2008
  636.72--dc22

                            2007031512

# CONTENTS

# COMBINATION CANINES

Ask five of your friends to describe their favorite dog. Chances are, each person will describe a very different dog. Choosing the right dog for you is important. Before deciding, you need to know what you want.

People have been looking for the perfect canine for more than 12,000 years. A canine is any animal that is part of the Canidae **family**.

Through the years, dog **breeders** have created hundreds of dog breeds. These dogs are called **purebred** dogs. Yet for some people, none of those purebreds is quite right. For these people, the answer may be a mix of two different purebreds.

Today, crosses between two different **purebred** dogs are called designer dogs. One of the most popular designer dogs is the schnoodle. Schnoodles are a mix of schnauzers and poodles.

*Crossing the popular schnauzer and poodle breeds has resulted in a handsome designer dog, the schnoodle!*

# SCHNAUZERS

There are three different **breeds** of schnauzers. Giant schnauzers are the largest breed. Miniature schnauzers are the smallest and most popular breed. And, standard schnauzers are the third breed.

Schnauzers have been popular pets since the 1400s. They were originally bred in Germany to hunt rats. They have also worked as watchdogs, guard dogs, and police dogs.

Today's schnauzers still make excellent watchdogs. They are brave and intelligent. Giant and standard schnauzers can herd and guard livestock as they did hundreds of years ago. And, miniature schnauzers can be good with children.

Many families like schnauzers because they have a low-shedding coat. And, they are easy to train.

Schnauzers also make loyal companions. Their loyalty can make them territorial, however. So, visitors may need to be cautious around a pet schnauzer.

*The standard schnauzer is the original breed. The giant and miniature breeds were bred from it long ago.*

# POODLES

Like schnauzers, poodles come in three sizes. However standard, miniature, and toy poodles are all considered a single **breed**.

It is believed the poodle originated in Germany in the 1500s. Early poodles were used to help duck hunters. As good swimmers, they could retrieve birds from water. Poodles made their way to the United States in the late 1800s.

This popular breed is known for being highly intelligent and easy to train. Poodles may perform tricks in a circus or simply for their owners. They also make excellent watchdogs.

When it comes to breeding designer dogs, poodles are popular because of their coats. Most dogs have fur that grows and then falls out, or

sheds. Shedding can cause big problems for people who are allergic to fur. But poodle coats grow long unless trimmed, much like human hair. So, poodles often do not bother people with such allergies.

**Poodles are well behaved with children and other pets.**

# SCHNOODLE HISTORY

No one knows who **bred** the original schnoodle. It is believed that schnoodles made their first appearance during the 1980s.

Early schnoodle breeders had big goals. They wanted to create a low-shedding family dog. Breeders also preferred a medium-sized dog. And, they wanted a dog with fewer health problems than most **purebred** dogs.

A purebred dog will likely have more health problems than a mixed-breed dog. A purebred puppy inherits the same genes from each parent. If those genes cause health problems, the puppy will also have health problems.

Crossing different **breeds** reduces the chances of passing on the same genes. Of course, crossbred puppies may still get some undesirable genes. For example, some schnoodles may shed if their coat takes after their schnauzer parent.

# SCHNOODLES

A schnoodle may be a good choice for someone who is allergic to dog fur. This is because both parent lines are low-shedding **breeds**. Schnoodles are also very intelligent. The smarter the dog, the easier it is to train!

It's also possible to breed schnoodles in different sizes to fit various needs. Someone in a small apartment may want a schnoodle bred from a toy poodle and a miniature schnauzer. A person living on a farm may want the puppy of a standard poodle and a giant schnauzer.

People may choose a schnoodle based on personality. They may like the look of a schnauzer but want a calmer dog. The influence of the poodle breed makes schnoodles less territorial than **purebred** schnauzers.

The schnoodle's intelligence makes it one of the easiest crossbreeds to train.  This fun-loving dog is eager to please its owner.

# BEHAVIOR

Schnoodle owners say their dogs are loving, loyal, happy, and protective. However, the personality of a particular schnoodle depends on its background.

Most schnoodles prefer to be the only pet in the house. And, they may be more comfortable with adults than with children. However, training can help with this. Training can also prevent schnoodles from barking too much.

Schnoodles can be quite active. They prefer their training to be active, too. These intelligent dogs can easily learn **agility** skills.

Some people have had success training schnoodles to hunt. This is not surprising since both schnauzers and poodles began as hunting dogs.

Once in a while, a schnoodle may cause problems by digging holes in the yard. This can be corrected with training, attention, and exercise.

*The quietest and most relaxed schnoodles are those with giant schnauzer and standard poodle parents.*

# Coats & Colors

A schnoodle coat is not quite as curly as a poodle coat. It is not as wiry as a schnauzer coat, either. Instead, it is soft and wavy.

Most schnoodles are gray, silver, or black. They can also be brown, white, or apricot. Some schnoodles have a white mask on their faces. Like schnauzers, some schnoodles develop a silvery coat as they age.

Commonly, the schnauzer genes are dominant. So, most schnoodles strongly resemble schnauzers. They have the schnauzer's square nose and its ear position. Schnoodles may also have a trace of the famous schnauzer mustache. But, the schnoodle's fine bones and legs are like the poodle.

A schnoodle needs frequent grooming. A stiff-toothed steel dog comb is essential for preventing knots in the schnoodle's coat.

# SIZES

A schnoodle's mother can be one of three different sizes. So can its father. That leads to a lot of variety in schnoodle sizes!

**Tiny schnoodle puppies are born blind and deaf. They are completely dependent on their mothers.**

Smaller schnoodles standing under 12 inches (30 cm) tall should weigh about 10 pounds (5 kg). Larger schnoodles may have a shoulder height of 15 inches (38 cm) or more. They usually weigh 13 to 20 pounds (6 to 9 kg).

The largest schnoodles have a slight health advantage. Dogs **bred** from giant schnauzers and standard poodles tend to have fewer health problems. They may also live longer than smaller schnoodles.

*For safety, a schnoodle should always wear a collar with identification tags.*

# CARE

Like all dogs, schnoodles need regular visits to a veterinarian. Schnoodle puppies need vaccinations to prevent common canine diseases. Later, owners who do not want to **breed** their schnoodles should have them **spayed** or **neutered**.

The veterinarian should also check for health problems common in poodles and schnauzers. These include problems with hips and knees. Skin conditions, **epilepsy**, and eye problems are also common in both schnoodle parent breeds.

Schnoodles with soft, wavy coats need weekly brushing. A weekly bath also helps, especially if allergies are a concern. Schnoodles with poodlelike coats require a haircut every 6 to 12 weeks.

When owners provide their schnoodles with loving care, they can expect their pets to live for 10 to 15 years.

Daily on-leash walks are recommended for schnoodles. A healthy diet, plenty of fresh water, and soft bedding are also important. Last but not least, schnoodles need lots of love and attention!

21

# GLOSSARY

**agility** - the ability to move quickly and easily.

**breed** - a group of animals sharing the same appearance and characteristics. A breeder is a person who raises animals. Raising animals is often called breeding them.

**epilepsy** - a disorder involving repeated seizures. Seizures are episodes of disturbed brain function that cause changes in attention and behavior.

**family** - a group that scientists use to classify similar plants or animals. It ranks above a genus and below an order.

**neuter** - to remove a male animal's reproductive organs.

**purebred** - an animal whose parents are both from the same breed.

**spay** - to remove a female animal's reproductive organs.

# WEB SITES

To learn more about designer dogs, visit ABDO Publishing Company on the World Wide Web at **www.abdopublishing.com**. Web sites about designer dogs are featured on our Book Links page. These links are routinely monitored and updated to provide the most current information available.

# INDEX

24